j746.92 H515b
Bchind
fa
H
D0624861

MAY 2 5 2017

WITHDRAWN

Behind the Glamour

BEHIND [THE] SCENES
FASHION CAREERS

By Susan Henneberg

CAPSTONE PRESS
a capstone imprint

Savvy Books are published by Capstone Press,
1710 Roe Crest Drive, North Mankato, Minnesota 56003
www.mycapstone.com

Copyright © 2017 by Capstone Press, a Capstone imprint. All rights reserved. No part of this publication may be reproduced in whole or in part, or stored in a retrieval system, or transmitted in any formor by any means, electronic, mechanical, photocopying, recording, or otherwise, without written permission of the publisher.

Library of Congress cataloging-in-publication data is available on the Library of Congress website

ISBN: 978-1-5157-4897-7 (hardcover) -- 978-1-5157-4910-3 (eBook PDF)

Summary: Fascinating facts, fun pictures, and easy-to-read sidebars highlight informative text about some of the most interesting jobs that take place behind the scenes in the fashion industry. Readers will get a glimpse at what it takes to make it as a retail buyer, stylist, fashion writer, and more and find out what goes on behind the glamour.

Editorial Credits:
Editor: Alison Deering
Designer: Heidi Thompson and Kayla Rossow
Media reseacher: Pam Mitsakos
Production specialist: Tori Abraham

Image Credits:
Alamy: Cliff Hide PR, 43 top right, Ovidiu Hrubaru, 40; Capstone Press: 44 top right; Getty Images: Beck Starr, 16 top right, BJI/Blue Jean Images, 22, Gabriel Olsen, 48 middle right, Hero Images, 12 top left, Jeffrey Mayer, 48 bottom right, Jordan Siemens, 53 middle left, Neil Mockford, 50 bottom left, Rolf Bruderer, 35 bottom right, Tasia Wells, 38 bottom middle; Newscom: Carlos Tischler/Splash News, 46 middle left; Shutterstock: Action Sports Photography, 33 top right, Africa Studio, 28 top, amixstudio, 25 bottom left, Andrey Armyagov, 33 top middle, Andrey_Popov, 24 top right, Andrii Kobryn, 17, Becky Starsmore, 19 top, Beer5020, 31 bottom middle, bikeriderlondon, 37, 39 top, 47, 56 bottom right, Blend Images, 12 bottom left, BlueSkyImage, 18 top right, BONNINSTUDIO, 9, 31 bottom right, Christophe Testi, 50 middle left, Comaniciu Dan, 14 top middle, Daniel Jedzura, 26 top right, Deborah Kolb, 49 bottom left, Deviant, 50 top middle, Diego Cervo, cover top left, 16 bottom right, Dikiiy, 44 bottom, Dmitry Kalinovsky, 60 middle left, Dragon Images, 24 middle, 43 bottom left, Eugenio Marongiu, 14 bottom left, 30 top left, fashionall, 38 top left, 38 top right, FashionStock.com, 4, 13, 18 middle left, 19 middle, 23 bottom right, 30 top right, Georgejmclittle, 55 bottom middle, Gina Smith, 57, goodluz, 58, GoodMood Photo, 55 bottom left, greenga, 14 middle left, 14 middle right, Iakov Filimonov, 36 middle right, 53 top left, 53 bottom left, Igor Bulgarin, 50 middle right, iofoto, 26 bottom right, Jaguar PS, 39 bottom, jgolby, 48 top left, Jordan Tan, 1, Karkas, 16 top, 33 middle, Kite_rin, 52, kubais, 18 bottom right, Lawrey, 27, lenetstan, 46 bottom right, leungchopan, 12 top right, lev radin, 61 bottom right, Liderina, 31 bottom left, MaleWitch, 10 left, meatbull, 23 bottom left, michaeljung, 54, Monkey Business Images, 6 top right, 34 top right, 42, 45 bottom right, 55 top left, Nejron Photo, 49 middle left, NemesisINC, cover bottom middle, Ollyy, 8, oneinchpunch, 61 middle right, Ovidiu Hrubaru, 28 bottom, 29 bottom, Pakawat Suwannaket, 33 bottom middle, Paul Matthew Photography, 46 bottom left, Pavel L Photo and Video, 21 bottom right, 26 top left, 51 bottom right, Pavel_dp, 20-21 top, Peter Bernik, 20 middle right, Photocrea, 24, bottom left, Photographee.eu, 7 top left, posteriori, 33 middle right, Preobrajenskiy, 38 bottom right, ProStockStudio, 60 middle right, racorn, 36 bottom left, Raisa Kanareva, 50 middle, Soloviova Liudmyla, 61 top left, SpeedKingz, 32, Syda Productions, 41 bottom left, Sylvie Bouchard, 11 top left, Tinxi, 10 bottom, Vagengeim, 7 top right, Vorobyeva, 6 bottom, Wallenrock, 21 bottom left, wavebreakmedia, cover top right, 6 top left, 15 top left, 29 top, 34 top left, 36 bottom right, 45 top right, 55 bottom right, 59, Yuganov Konstantin, 5, Yulia Reznikov, 30 bottom right; Thinkstock: gpointstudio, 38 middle left

Design Elements: Capstone Studio: Karon Dubke; Shutterstock: helen-light, Jozef Sowa, Le Panda, optimarc

Source Credits: p. 12 from www.shopify.com/guides/ultimate-guide-to-pop-up-shops and "Visual Merchandiser." Careers at H&M. Video; p. 14 from www.cosmopolitan.com/career/interviews/a46165/get-that-life-rebecca-minkoff-fashion; p. 16 from courtneyallegra.com/magento/index.php/press/full-articles.html and Patricia Wooster, *So You Want to Work in Fashion*, New York: Aladdin, 2014; p. 21 from www.harpersbazaar.com/culture/features/a10705/charlotte-tilbury-0515 and www.intothegloss.com/2013/05/charlotte-tilbury-makeup-artist; p. 25 from Patrick Demarchelier, *The Teen Vogue Handbook*, New York: Razorbill, 2009; p. 28 from www.adweek.com/news/advertising-branding/16-year-old-media-mogul-tavi-gevinson-expanding-her-empire; p. 30 from www.thedailybeast.com/articles/2012/05/15/tyra-banks-open-letter-to-models-vogue-to-images-of-anorexia; p. 34 from Amy Astley, *The Teen Vogue Handbook*, New York: Razorbill, 2009; p. 38 from Nick Wooster, *So You Want to Work in Fashion?*, New York: Aladdin, 2014; p. 39 from www.teenvogue.com/story/how-to-be-celebrity-stylist; p. 40 from Rachel Zoe, *Living in Style*, New York: Grand Central Life Style, 2014, and www.complex.com/style/2013/04/how-to-make-it-tips-for-becoming-a-fashion-stylist; p. 41 from www.exclusivelyfashionmag.com/stories/stories2011/exstories2011-6nchavez; p. 43 from Patricia Wooster, *So You Want to Work in Fashion*; p. 44 from www.cosmopolitan.com/career/interviews/a48880/get-that-life-aya-kanai-project-runway-junior; p. 49 from the.hitchcock.zone/wiki/American_Film_(1978)_-_Dialogue_on_Film:_Edith_Head; p. 54 from www.complex.com/style/2012/01/10-entry-level-jobs-in-the-fashion-industry; p. 59 from Gloria Baume, *The Teen Vogue Handbook*, New York: Razorbill, 2009; p. 61 from www.cosmopolitan.com/career/a53838/aimee-cheshire-hey-gorgeous-get-that-life and www.cosmopolitan.com/career/interviews/a46165/get-that-life-rebecca-minkoff-fashion

Printed in Canada.
010039S17

Table of Contents

"I DON'T DO FASHION. I AM FASHION."
— COCO CHANEL

Introduction

If you're like many teens, a career in the glamorous world of fashion sounds like a dream come true. Strutting down the runway in a killer designer dress. Snapping photographs of famous models as they hit the catwalk. Hitting the trendy stores to style a famous celeb. The fashion industry can provide great career options for people who have a strong sense of style and love clothes. However, it can be competitive. Like you, thousands of teens want to be a *Vogue* supermodel or a *Project Runway* winner. Only a handful make it to the top every year. The good news is the fashion world is huge, and there are plenty of jobs to be found behind the glamour.

If you have a passion for fashion, then you have much in common with many of today's successful designers, photographers, and stylists. While still teens, they sewed their own clothes. They devoured fashion magazines and blogs. They worked in retail. They saved to study fashion in college or trade school. There they learned about the wide range of occupations in the fashion industry.

You might be interested in the more creative side of the fashion world. If so, you can become a designer, photographer, display designer, makeup artist, or stylist. Maybe you love to talk about fashion with your friends, which could lead to a career in fashion writing and public relations. Or perhaps you're fascinated by the business side of fashion. You might think about being part of buying, production, and sales.

How do you choose which field is right for you? First things first — find out what you are passionate about. Earn a degree or certification in a fashion-related field. Get experience as an intern or an assistant. Work hard, ask questions, and take risks. There are huge opportunities in the fashion industry. It's a big, exciting world, just waiting for smart, creative, ambitious people like you!

CHAPTER 1
Display Designer

As you walk by your favorite store, do the windows ever make you do a double take? Do the displays make you want to rush inside and try on the clothes? If so, you have fallen for the magic of display designers and visual merchandisers. A display designer's job is to get you into the store. Once they've made a good first impression, they want you to stay and buy. How do they do that? It's all about telling the story.

Display designers pay close attention to what's going on in the fashion world. They have one eye on celebrity social media feeds and the other on fashion magazine spreads. They predict what shoppers will want to wear each season. And they make sure the store mannequins rock the latest trends. Display designers don't just want to sell you the top or the jeans or the cute jacket that pulls the look together — they want you to buy the whole outfit!

Visual displays reflect some kind of theme, such as spring break or an upcoming holiday. In large national chain stores, the head office assigns the themes. The branch stores then get detailed instructions on how to put together the displays. Designers often find creative ways to connect the clothes to your lifestyle. A mannequin wearing shorts, a crop top, and carrying a tote full of accessories tells you it's time to get outfitted for a beach getaway.

Display designers also create displays for apparel companies at trade shows — large conventions with hundreds of booths. Each booth showcases products from different companies. At the annual New York Shoe Expo, for example, more than 300 footwear makers show off different brands of shoes. At trade shows, designers have more creative power — they come up with inventive themes and eye-catching arrangements to make their employers' goods stand out. Their job is to sell their clothing, shoe, or accessory label to store buyers.

BOOTHS AT SI' SPOSAITALIA
EXHIBITION IN MILAN

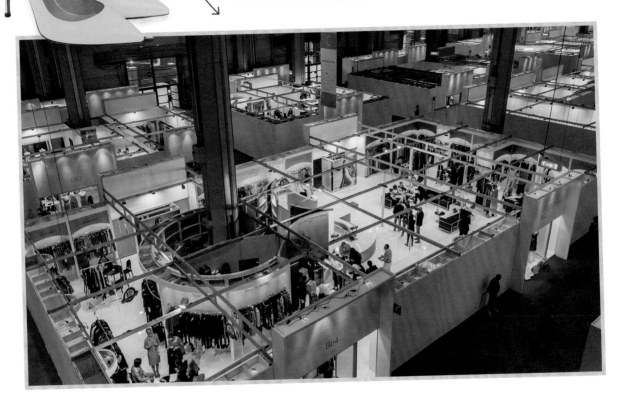

So how can you break into this creative field? As with most careers in fashion, you need to be prepared to start as an intern or assistant to more experienced designers. A college degree in art or fashion merchandising will give you an edge in getting hired and moving up. For now, get a head start by taking a closer look at the displays at your favorite stores. See if you can figure out what the display designers did to catch your eye. What story are they trying to tell?

At a Glance

The basics: Display designer

Also known as: Fashion merchandiser

Overview: Display designers plan commercial displays to entice and appeal to customers. They change or rotate window displays, interior display areas, or signage to reflect promotions or changes in inventory.

Education/skills required: Training in vocational schools, related on-the-job experience, or an associate's degree

Suggested courses: Art, interior design, stagecraft, introduction to business

Salary range: $24,580–$92,470/year

Median salary: $26.40/hour or $54,920/year

FIRST PERSON: SHOPIFY

"Whether you're a small business retailer or planning your first pop-up store, your window display is one of the most powerful weapons. . . . This is your chance to . . . turn the heads of those passing by and engage them enough to stop, look back, and walk in to your store where your floor staff or products can sweep them off their feet and get them to make a purchase."

— Humayan Khan, visual merchandiser
at online shopping website Shopify

> IT'S NOT ALL ABOUT STYLING AND PICKING CLOTHES. YOU HAVE TO BE HANDY. IN MY DEPARTMENT I'M WORKING WITH WINDOWS, AND WE HAVE TO CARRY MANNEQUINS UP LADDERS. WE HAVE TO BUILD, DRILL, SPACKLE, AND PAINT. IT'S A LITTLE CONSTRUCTION, A LITTLE ASSEMBLY, A LITTLE OF EVERYTHING.
>
> —V. ORPIANO, VISUAL MERCHANDISER AT H&M

CHAPTER 2

Fashion Designer

Do you imagine seeing clothes you designed coming down the runway during Fashion Week? Or picture your shoes and accessories gracing the pages of your favorite magazine? If so, fashion design might be the career for you. Fashion design is one of the most glamorous careers in the fashion industry. It's also competitive. But don't let that discourage you. Fashion is a huge industry, and designers are needed for many areas, including footwear, accessories, jewelry, wedding gowns, and dozens of others.

Fashion design begins with a vision and a sketchbook. Designers do their homework before starting to sketch. They learn trends and find out what their customers want. They visit trade shows to find out what sells. Then they give their detailed sketches to the production team, which creates samples to show buyers.

Most new designers work for large companies — stores such as Gap, Target, or J.C. Penney. In these mass-production businesses, hundreds of designs are quickly produced, marketed, and sold. Most of the time the design house's name is on the label rather than the designer's. Some designers hope to move up into ready-to-wear clothing for stores such as Nordstrom or Macy's. There, designs will be more exclusive and marketed to upscale customers. Others hope to get into couture, where one-of-a-kind designs are made.

> I FEEL LIKE AS A DESIGNER, YOU NEED TO BE ABLE TO COMMUNICATE AND WORK WITH PEOPLE. YOU DON'T HAVE TO BE AN EXPERT IN ALL AREAS, BUT YOU HAVE TO KNOW HOW TO DO ALL OF THEM. IF I HAD SOME FINANCIAL EDUCATION OR BASICS ABOUT A BUSINESS, THAT WOULD HAVE BEEN REALLY HELPFUL.
>
> – REBECCA MINKOFF, FASHION DESIGNER

If you're a budding designer, consider attending an art or fashion school. There you can build a fashion background and develop your skills. Internships are also a great way to gain practical experience and valuable networking contacts. Beginning designers usually start as assistants to designers before developing their own lines. Those who are creative and original can find a rewarding career turning their visions into reality.

At a Glance

The basics: Fashion designer

Overview: Fashion designers create original clothing, accessories, and footwear. They sketch designs, select fabrics and patterns, and give instructions on how to produce the products they design.

Education requirements: Bachelor's degree in art or fashion design

Suggested courses: Art, clothing design and sewing, computer-assisted design (CAD), drawing and painting, textiles, introduction to business

Salary range: $33,170–$125,270/year

Median salary: $30.61/hour or $63,670/year

FIRST PERSON: BIKINI PRODIGY

What's it like to become a fashion sensation while still in high school? "Bikini Prodigy" Courtney Allegra turned her dreams of becoming a fashion designer into reality before she was 18 years old. Called "fun and flirty," Allegra's line of swimsuits has been featured in *Seventeen* magazine as well as on the *TODAY* show and *Pretty Little Liars*.

"As far as swimwear goes, I inspired myself to start designing simply because I couldn't find the "perfect bikini," Allegra told *SuperFab* magazine in 2015. Next up for her is a new line of men's swimwear.

> **"** THE MOST IMPORTANT THING YOUNG DESIGNERS CAN DO IS BECOME AWARE OF THE WORLD AROUND THEM. THEY SHOULD BE INSPIRED BY THEIR ENVIRONMENT AND IMMERSE THEMSELVES IN CULTURE. TRAVEL; GO TO MUSEUMS; SEE FASHION EXHIBITIONS; STUDY FILM, COSTUMES, AND MUSIC – EVERY ASPECT OF THE WORLD SHOULD SERVE AS INSPIRATION AND SPARK CREATIVITY.
>
> – MARY STEPHENS, DIRECTOR OF FASHION DESIGN AT FIDM **"**

CHAPTER 3

Fashion Makeup Artist

If you've ever spent hours in front of the mirror carefully applying makeup, you know the skill required. Makeup artists can change an everyday look into anything from red carpet glam to street style punk. They are an essential part of any fashion team. No model would appear on the runway or in a magazine photo shoot without carefully designed makeup to complete the look.

A day in the life of a makeup artist is never boring — largely because it's never the same. As a makeup artist working in the fashion industry, you might spend a morning making up the models for a local magazine fashion spread. In the afternoon you may be working on location for a TV commercial. In the evening, you could be working backstage at a runway show.

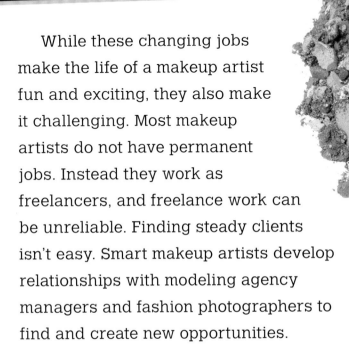

While these changing jobs make the life of a makeup artist fun and exciting, they also make it challenging. Most makeup artists do not have permanent jobs. Instead they work as freelancers, and freelance work can be unreliable. Finding steady clients isn't easy. Smart makeup artists develop relationships with modeling agency managers and fashion photographers to find and create new opportunities.

Makeup artists are in especially high demand during major fashion weeks. Lead makeup artists meet with fashion designers and stylists ahead of runway shows in order to develop themes and looks. They apply makeup on a demo model for the rest of the artists to copy. Fashion week makeup artists learn to apply makeup quickly and accurately despite the stress and hectic pace fashion week brings.

ALL ABOUT MICHELLE PHAN

It's hard to believe that makeup mogul Michelle Phan was once rejected for a job at a department store makeup counter. So she began filming herself applying such looks as Snow White, Lady Gaga, and geisha. By 2016 more than eight million subscribers were regularly tuning into her YouTube channel for makeup tutorials. Her popularity created opportunities for Phan. She created a makeup line called *em* and a beauty subscription service called *ipsy*. She films her videos, and the videos of the dozens of YouTube stars she mentors, in her own Southern California studio. Her biggest accomplishment? Allowing her mother to retire.

There are many ways to prepare for the fast-paced, creative career of a fashion makeup artist. Practice at home by following your favorite beauty vloggers. Work at a makeup counter or in a beauty retailer to gain valuable experience. Attend cosmetology school to learn the basics of makeup. Even with practical skills and experience, be prepared to start as an intern or assistant. With talent and hard work, you will soon be on your way to an exciting career as a fashion makeup artist.

At a Glance

The basics: Fashion makeup artist

Overview: Makeup artists apply makeup for anyone appearing in front of a camera or live audience in film, television, theater, concerts, photographic sessions, or fashion shows.

Education/skills required: Cosmetology license recommended

Suggested courses: Cosmetology, drama, film, photography, stagecraft, introduction to business

Salary range: $22,850–$117,720/year

Median salary: $32.49/hour or $67,580/year

A DAY IN THE LIFE: MAKEUP ARTIST CHARLOTTE TILBURY SHARES HER DAY

6:00 a.m. I sleep in my makeup. I'm never, ever seen without it.

6:30 a.m. I start to get dressed. I live in high heels — I've got maybe 300 pairs.

7:30 a.m. I have to be at a show at least two hours in advance. I bring six suitcases full of makeup — better safe than sorry.

1:30 p.m. At lunch I might discuss up-and-coming products, counter reviews, or marketing with my team. I basically have a mobile office.

4:30 p.m. I have to juggle meetings all the time. Today I have a meeting with an editor. We're launching my brand in Canada in June because the line is quickly expanding.

8:00 p.m. Finally I have time to relax with my friends.

1:30 a.m. I fall asleep quite easily because I'm exhausted. Live life to the fullest and make the most of yourself with makeup — that's my mantra.

"BEAUTY IS POWER, AND MAKEUP IS SOMETHING THAT REALLY ENHANCES THAT; IT'S A WOMAN'S SECRET."
— CHARLOTTE TILBURY

21

CHAPTER 4

Fashion Photographer

Photographer Mario Testino knows exactly when his star began to rise in the fashion world: "Gucci made the fashion world look at me. Diana made the whole world look at me," he says, referring to the day he photographed the beloved British princess. While most fashion photographers don't have A-list clients such as Testino's, they can still earn a living doing the creative work they love.

Much like fashion makeup artists, fashion photographers typically work on a freelance basis. They may have an agent to help them find jobs and they network to find new clients. Ad agencies, shopping centers, and catalog companies all hire photographers to feature their products. One day a photographer may be shooting sunset photos of glamorous models. They next day, he or she might be in the studio for a catalog shoot, photographing one pair of shoes after another, making each look trendy and unique.

TYPES OF FASHION PHOTOGRAPHY

Fashion photographs fall into three main categories: commercial, editorial, and high fashion. Commercial images are all about selling the clothes. Outfits can be seen clearly and in detail. The models' makeup and hair tend to be simple so the clothes take center stage. Editorial photographs are found in fashion magazines. They tell a story about the clothes in a series of shots on a specific location. For instance, the models wear dreamy, romantic clothing in an old castle or fun beach styles on a tropical island. In high-fashion photography, photographers shoot top models posing dramatically in a fantasy wardrobe. Open the next issue of your favorite fashion magazine and see if you can identify each category.

But there is more to being a successful fashion photographer than just shooting photos. Photographers spend as much time in front of their computers as they do their cameras. They download their photos. Then they sift through them, choosing the best. They use editing software to brighten shadows, correct the color, and change backlight effects.

As a fashion photographer, you'll also need to know how to manage your business. Photographers are responsible for keeping their own accounts, which includes billing clients and paying fashion teams and lighting technicians. Equipment costs must also be accounted for, and they can be extensive. Most fashion work is done with digital single lens reflex cameras. A beginning camera can range from $3,000 to $8,000. Lenses, studio lights, computer hardware, and software

also add to the cost of doing business. A pro can easily spend $35,000 on the high-quality equipment needed to produce images for magazines, billboards, and websites.

CAMERA

LENS

At a Glance

The basics: Fashion photographer

Overview: A fashion photographer takes pictures of people, landscapes, merchandise, or other subjects, using digital or film cameras and equipment. He or she may develop negatives or use computer software to produce finished images and prints. Fashion photographers select the sites and backgrounds for photo shoots, help models pose to capture the best features of clothing items, and choose which photographs to feature.

Education/skills required: Training in vocational schools, related on-the-job experience, or an associate's degree

Suggested courses: Art, film, photography, entrepreneurship

Salary range: $18,850–$72,000/year

Median salary: $15.24/hour or $31,710/year

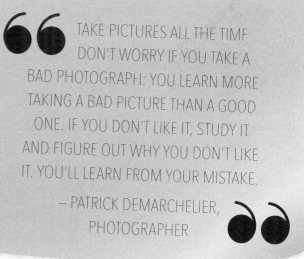

66 TAKE PICTURES ALL THE TIME. DON'T WORRY IF YOU TAKE A BAD PHOTOGRAPH: YOU LEARN MORE TAKING A BAD PICTURE THAN A GOOD ONE. IF YOU DON'T LIKE IT, STUDY IT AND FIGURE OUT WHY YOU DON'T LIKE IT. YOU'LL LEARN FROM YOUR MISTAKE.

– PATRICK DEMARCHELIER, PHOTOGRAPHER 99

Fashion photographers get their start in a variety of ways. Some take a photography course at an art school. Others earn a college art degree. Almost all assist established photographers to learn the tricks of the trade and build their portfolios.

CREATING A PORTFOLIO

A portfolio of your best photos is the most important tool for a photographer trying to break into the fashion world. A website can showcase many photos for little money. However, most potential employers want to see what they call "your book." To make your book, print at least 20 good-quality photos measuring 4 x 5 inches. Have a variety of shots. You will want close-up portraits, groups of people, and scenes. Above all, photo editors say, allow your personality to come through.

CHAPTER 5

Fashion Writer

Do you love reading fashion magazines? Do you dream of seeing your writing in the pages of *Vogue, Marie Claire*, or *Glamour*? With more than 200 different fashion magazines in print every month, that dream could become a reality. The fashion industry needs writers. The magazines you see gracing bookstore shelves, magazine racks, and newsstands are the oldest and most visible source of jobs, but there are many others. Trade journals such as *Women's Wear Daily* and *Accessories* magazine hire writers to keep fashion insiders informed.

Print magazines aren't the only option for fashion writers, either. Most print magazines have websites that allow writers to post instant updates and breaking fashion news. Newspapers, reality shows, and design house blogs also need writers and editors to create their fashion content. The most up-and-coming fashion writers run their own blogs. Some bloggers are even turning their passion for documenting their fashion lifestyles into full-time careers. Top bloggers can attract millions of followers to their websites. Thanks to their online presence, they're able to earn solid incomes from their websites, personal appearances, and product endorsements.

STYLE ROOKIE

Tavi Gavinson was only 11 when she started her blog *Style Rookie*. In frequent posts, she showed off her quirky, unique style. The next thing she knew, she was sitting next to *Vogue* editor Anna Wintour at New York Fashion Week. She has been featured in *Teen Vogue* and starred in a video for fashion label Rodarte. Gavinson now edits an online magazine called *Rookie*. The site invites readers, including Sarah Silverman and Lena Dunham, to contribute writing, photography, and other art. Gavinson's philosophy? "I think that fashion can be a tool of feminism and of self-expression and individuality and empowerment."

So how can you get started as a fashion writer? You'll need a college degree to break into this field. Graduates with degrees in both journalism and fashion or a fashion-related field will have an edge.

You should also expect to work at least one internship as you get started. Most new writers start as interns and help their editors with many tasks. As you move up in the field, you'll have more input on what stories to include and which topics to focus on. Experienced fashion writers craft articles about fashion houses and explain new trends. They interview hot, up-and-coming designers. They also cover fashion shows and events. Keep in mind that even if a story doesn't seem groundbreaking, it's still important. Beginning writers need to get clips — stories with your name as a byline.

66

VOGUE HAS THE POWER TO
MAKE AND BREAK — WHETHER
IT'S FASHION TRENDS, DESIGNERS, MODELS,
AND YES, EVEN INDUSTRY PRACTICES.

— TYRA BANKS, SUPERMODEL
AND MEDIA MOGUL

99

VOGUE AS A TRENDSETTER

Most people working in fashion consider *Vogue* to be the most influential fashion magazine in the industry, if not the world. *Vogue* began in 1892 as a weekly newspaper for the elite of New York society and has been in print for more than 120 years. Publisher Condé Nast exported the magazine to Britain and the rest of Europe in the 1910s and 1920s. Now Anna Wintour, *Vogue*'s editor-in-chief, calls the magazine everyone's "glamorous girlfriend." Its September issues often exceed 600 pages.

At a Glance

The basics: Fashion writer

Also known as: Fashion journalist

Overview: Fashion writers create features and copy for a variety of media outlets including fashion magazines, advertising and trade publications, newspapers, blogs, and online magazines.

Education/skills required: Bachelor's degree in journalism, communications, fashion design, fashion merchandising

Suggested courses: Communications, computer applications, journalism, public speaking

Salary range: $29,230–$114,530/year

Median salary: $33.24/hour or $69,130/year

"YOU EITHER KNOW FASHION OR YOU DON'T."
— ANNA WINTOUR

CHAPTER 6
Retail Buyer

Sure you love shopping — who doesn't? — but what is it like to actually buy clothes for a living? Retail buyers attend fashion shows. They travel the globe searching for new trends. They rub shoulders with famous designers. But being a retail buyer isn't all glamour. Making sure a store carries items that will sell is a big responsibility. Buyers have to choose the right garments. They have to get the right sizes, quantities, and prices. To do that, they need to know the customers they are buying for.

There are several kinds of retail buyers. Buyers for large, national chain stores such as Macy's and Bloomingdales specialize in one area. Some focus on dresses. Others handle junior sportswear or shoes. Buyers for fast-fashion stores such as Forever 21, Zara, and Topshop, where new styles arrive weekly, have to stay on top of designer looks for their on-trend customers. Buyers in smaller independent stores need to be knowledgeable in all areas, from men's suits to children's clothes.

OPPORTUNITIES FOR TEENS: FASHION SUMMER PROGRAMS

How would you like to get a head start on a career in fashion? Many fashion colleges open their doors during the summer to high school students. The Rhode Island School of Design, Fashion Institute of Technology, and LIM all offer summer programs and have a wide variety of majors. You can learn about design, photography, and writing. Parsons takes its summer class to Paris. If you are in middle school, you can take classes in fashion design at the Parsons campus in New York. For young California fashionistas, FDIM gives crash courses in the fashion industry at any of its campuses across the state. Aspiring fashion writers can apply to the *New York Times* summer program in "The Future of Fashion." If you are in the United Kingdom, you can attend programs in fashion design, photography, styling, and media at the London College of Fashion. If traveling to the major fashion hubs is out of the question, look closer to home. Just about every fashion or art school recruits teens for summer programs.

Regardless of what type of store they work for, retail buyers all have two main goals. They need to buy goods that the store can sell at a profit, and they need to keep customers coming back for more. One of the most challenging parts of the job is predicting what customers will want. Buyers must work at least six months in advance. In order to predict trends, they read trade magazines and attend trade shows. They talk to designers and publicists. They meet with manufacturers. Good buyers keep an eye on celebrity trendsetters. They watch what is selling in other stores or websites and analyze what has sold in the past.

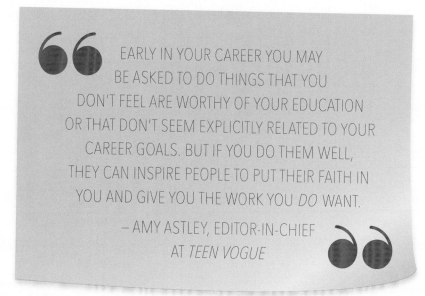

> EARLY IN YOUR CAREER YOU MAY BE ASKED TO DO THINGS THAT YOU DON'T FEEL ARE WORTHY OF YOUR EDUCATION OR THAT DON'T SEEM EXPLICITLY RELATED TO YOUR CAREER GOALS. BUT IF YOU DO THEM WELL, THEY CAN INSPIRE PEOPLE TO PUT THEIR FAITH IN YOU AND GIVE YOU THE WORK YOU *DO* WANT.
>
> – AMY ASTLEY, EDITOR-IN-CHIEF AT *TEEN VOGUE*

At a Glance

The basics: Retail buyer

Overview: Fashion buyers purchase women's, men's, and children's clothing and accessories for both retail and wholesale stores.

Education/skills required: Bachelor's degree in buying and merchandising, general business, purchasing and contracts management

Suggested courses: Accounting, computer applications, introduction to business, marketing, principles of sales, retail marketing

Salary range: $30,200–$95,590/year

Median salary: $25.45/hour or $52,940/year

So how can you get paid to shop for a living? There are lots of things you can do right now to increase your chances of getting hired as a retail buyer. If your school offers job shadowing or internships, see if you can arrange one with a local store buyer. Consider an after-school or summer job in an apparel store to learn the business.

When it comes time for college, major in fashion merchandising, business, or finance. These degrees will give you an edge with hiring managers. With the right experience and education, you can turn your love for buying clothes into a fun and successful career.

A FASHIONABLE EDUCATION

Where's the best place to learn the ins and outs of the fashion industry? There are many prestigious fashion schools including Parsons School of Design, LIM, Fashion Institute of Technology (FIT), Pratt Institute in New York, and the Fashion Institute of Design & Merchandising (FDIM) in California. There are good schools in other parts of the world as well. Fashion students should consider the Savannah College of Art and Design in Georgia, Kent State University in Ohio, Drexel University in Philadelphia, and Iowa State University. And don't rule out community colleges — many offer associate's degrees in apparel design or merchandising. There are also many top fashion schools in the United Kingdom. Central Saint Martins, Kingston University, and the University of Westminster are all in London. For international flair, consider Polimoda in Florence, Italy, or Bunka Fashion College in Tokyo. Fashion experts emphasize that the particular school is not as important as the passion, energy, and creativity that the graduates bring to a job.

CHAPTER 7

Stylist

Ever wondered how models in fashion magazines look totally chic and pulled together? Or how celebrities always seem perfectly styled on social media? What you are looking at is the work of fashion stylists. A stylist's job is to make his or her clients look their best. Many aspire to dress A-list clients with fashions from top designers. Styling is a fast-paced, exciting world, however, it's also a difficult field to break into. Fortunately, there are many opportunities to gain experience right in your own community.

A stylist's life is often a whirlwind of fashion-related activity. Attending trade shows and exhibitions, browsing fashion magazines and websites, keeping an eye on designer and celebrity social media feeds — all are necessary parts of the job. Creating and maintaining a client's personal style takes a talent for organization and attention to detail. As stylists create original looks for their clients, they also create their lookbook — a portfolio of photographs or magazine tear sheets in which their looks have been featured. A professional lookbook is a stylist's visual resumé.

> 66 THE TWO THINGS I REQUIRE BEFORE I WOULD EVEN MEET WITH SOMEONE IS AN ACTIVE SOCIAL MEDIA PRESENCE AND EXPERIENCE WORKING IN RETAIL. YOU HAVE TO BE INVOLVED IN RETAIL, IN MY OPINION, IN ORDER TO BE SUCCESSFUL.
>
> – NICK WOOSTER, MENSWEAR AUTHORITY AND J.C. PENNEY CREATIVE ADVISOR

"FASHION FADES, STYLE IS ETERNAL."

– YVES SAINT LAURENT

Fashion stylists are needed in a variety of places. You might work as a stylist or personal shopper in a store, putting together professional looks or perfect outfits for special occasions. You might be needed to create looks for catalogs or print ads. Photographers need stylists to dress models for photo shoots. Local news stations, wedding planners, and ad agencies all need stylists to create unique style images.

ADVICE FROM A PRO

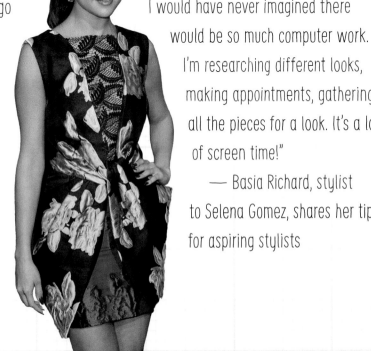

"Internships teach you how to start a job, how to finish the job, how to go from the show room to costume houses. When I was an intern for a stylist, I got to work with celebrities like Jeremy Piven and Christina Aguilera. From there, I started to put my lookbook together and was able to work my own jobs and get clients on my own, such as Selena Gomez. . . . I would have never imagined there would be so much computer work. I'm researching different looks, making appointments, gathering all the pieces for a look. It's a lot of screen time!"

— Basia Richard, stylist to Selena Gomez, shares her tips for aspiring stylists

How can you land a job as a stylist? Most start as an assistant to a more established stylist. Or they intern as part of a fashion merchandising or fashion design degree. A background in fashion retailing can also help you get a foot in the door. Courses in business or accounting will be useful, as most fashion stylists are self-employed. If you want to work with celebrities, be prepared to relocate to the star capitals of the world — Los Angeles, California; New York City; London, England; or Paris, France. Wherever you land, spending your days making people look their best could be the perfect career for you.

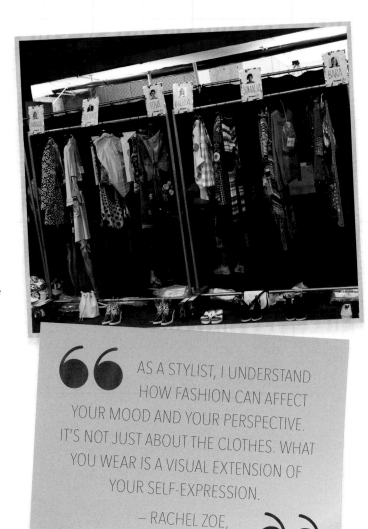

66 AS A STYLIST, I UNDERSTAND HOW FASHION CAN AFFECT YOUR MOOD AND YOUR PERSPECTIVE. IT'S NOT JUST ABOUT THE CLOTHES. WHAT YOU WEAR IS A VISUAL EXTENSION OF YOUR SELF-EXPRESSION.

– RACHEL ZOE, CELEBRITY STYLIST 99

GETTING THE DETAILS RIGHT

"Even if you don't go to school for fashion, there are a few easy ways to learn about the details. Most people live near department stores, and if you're lucky, there's probably even a high-end boutique you can get to. Compare pants and shirts you own to the pricier stuff, and really try to notice the differences in cuts and design. Turn those same garments inside out to see how they're made. Chop it up with different associates who seem to know the product, and learn what makes it 'good.' As you see more and more clothes from different designers you'll know your Balmain from your Balenciaga without having to look at the tags."

— Mathew Hensons, fashion editor for Complex Media, talks about designer clothes

At a Glance

The basics: Stylist

Also known as: Photographic stylist, wardrobe stylist, fashion stylist

Overview: A stylist is a consultant who selects the clothing for published editorial features, print or television advertising campaigns, music videos, concert performances, and any public appearances made by celebrities or other public figures.

Education/skills required: College degree in fashion design recommended

Suggested courses: Fashion design and/or merchandising, communications, marketing, art history, or photography

Salary range: $34,059–$79,463/year

Median salary: $49,263/year

" IT'S IMPORTANT THAT YOU KNOW FABRIC, IT'S IMPORTANT THAT YOU KNOW TEARING AND PATTERN MAKING. IT'S REALLY VALUABLE, BECAUSE A LOT OF THE TIME YOU WILL END UP REDESIGNING OR CO-DESIGNING. MY CLIENTS ARE SO INCREDIBLY BEAUTIFUL, BUT THEY'RE USUALLY NOT 6'0 MODELS. THEY ARE ACTRESSES AND THEY HAVE PERSONALITY, SO FOR EACH ONE YOU KIND OF HAVE TO CUSTOM FIT THE GOWNS TO THEM.

— NICOLE CHAVEZ, CELEBRITY STYLIST, SPEAKING TO *EXCLUSIVELY FASHION* MAGAZINE "

CHAPTER 8
Fashion Marketing & Public Relations

Where do design, sales, and journalism come together to form one amazing career? Fashion marketing and public relations (PR) professionals are found on the front lines of the fashion industry. If you are outgoing, creative, and a strong communicator, fashion PR may be the perfect place for you.

As a PR specialist, your role is to act as the face of the fashion label you represent and work hard to make that brand successful. To do that, you need to get your products in front of customers. Successful PR specialists organize product launches. They plan fashion shows and in-store events. They ask designers to talk to the media. They interact with fashion editors to get their products in magazines and on websites and collaborate with stylists who use their product line.

ADVICE FOR ASPIRING PR PROFESSIONALS

"Learn as much as you can about the industry by taking advantage of all the great fashion industry publications available to you online. Start a blog; write about the brands you love. Grab friends and spend the weekend doing crazy photo shoots. Learn photography; learn to edit those photos. Take classes in coding and graphic design. Don't wait for permission — just start your own thing."

— Crosby Noricks, creator of online fashion
public relations site PR Couture

> 66 DURING MY JUNIOR-YEAR SUMMER, I WAS AN INTERN AT *NEW YORK* MAGAZINE IN THE FASHION DEPARTMENT. AT THAT TIME, THE FASHION DEPARTMENT WAS VERY SMALL. THE FASHION DIRECTOR THERE WAS A REALLY INSPIRING PERSON. I LEARNED THAT YOU GET REWARDED WHEN YOU'RE AN INTERN BY BEING THE HARDEST-WORKING PERSON IN THE ROOM. I REALIZED SHE WOULD REWARD ME BY HELPING ME LEARN HOW THE FASHION INDUSTRY WORKS.
>
> — AYA KANI, FASHION DIRECTOR, *COSMOPOLITAN* AND *SEVENTEEN*

To make it as a marketing or public relations professional, you'll need top-notch communication skills. Publicists need to be confident speakers. They need to write clear, persuasive blog posts and press releases. You'll also need an active social media presence. An important part of a publicist's job is managing blogs and social media accounts. For many publicists, their brand's Instagram feed is as vital as its presence in *Vogue*.

So how can you get started now? Look for opportunities to speak and write about topics you're passionate about. Check out job shadowing or internships with a PR professional. Research colleges with courses focused on fashion marketing and public relations. Follow your favorite clothing brands or designers on social media, and take note of the strategies they use to grab your attention. When the time comes to launch your career as a PR professional in the fashion industry, you'll be ready to jump in head first.

INTERNSHIPS: A FOOT IN THE DOOR

Whether it's at a store, a design studio, or a fashion label, internships are especially vital in the fashion industry. Student interns often work for no pay, but they gain huge rewards in experience and valuable contacts. They get to network with industry professionals. Most interns also get

college credit toward their degrees — they typically work several days each week, which allows them to attend classes the other days. If you're lucky and work hard, an internship could turn into an entry-level position after graduation.

At a Glance

The basics: Fashion marketing specialist

Also known as: Public relations specialist, PR specialist

Overview: Marketing managers plan and execute the best ways to promote their employer's products, services, or brands.

Education/skills required: Bachelor's degree in marketing or public relations

Suggested courses: Accounting, banking and finance, computer applications, economics, introduction to business, marketing, psychology, statistics

Salary range: $31,690–$110,080/year

Median salary: $27.29/hour or $56,770/year

OUTDOOR FASHION SHOW PREPARATION

46

CHAPTER 9

Costume Designer

Costume designers have one of the coolest jobs in the fashion industry. They create designs for theater, dance, opera, circus, concerts, television, film, and theme parks. Sometimes they translate comic book figures into movie superheroes. Or they re-create the country life of 1920s British aristocracy. Cinderella, Big Bird, and Beyoncé have all been transformed because of the work of a costume designer.

If you love history, literature, and theater, costume design would be a great career for you. To accurately re-create the fashions of a historical period, you'd need to know all about the life and customs of the time — everything from clothing to shoes to accessories. You need to know how people dressed and how they styled their outfits to fit the time and their lifestyles.

COSTUME DESIGNERS GUILD AWARDS

On one special day each year, the Costume Designers Guild (CDG) rolls out the red carpet to celebrate artists' achievements. This association protects and improves the status of costume designers. The CDG gives awards to costume designers for motion pictures, television, and commercials. Past winners in film include the costume designers for *Mad Max: Fury Road*, *Into the Woods*, and *The Hunger Games: Catching Fire*. Television costume designers have won awards for *Game of Thrones*, *Downton Abbey*, and *Glee*.

TRISH SUMMERVILLE, COSTUME DESIGNER FOR *THE HUNGER GAMES: CATCHING FIRE*

For some costumes, a knowledge of the human anatomy is essential. Costumes have to be fashioned so that performers can actively move, which may require you to use different kinds of materials. For instance, designers use a special fabric for superheroes so the performers don't get too hot. Other costumes require special fasteners so that performers can quickly get in and out of them. Collaboration skills are also essential — it's up to the costume designers and the director to create a shared vision of the characters, brought to life by the costumes.

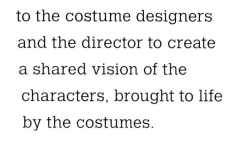

> " WHAT A COSTUME DESIGNER DOES IS A CROSS BETWEEN MAGIC AND CAMOUFLAGE. WE CREATE THE ILLUSION OF CHANGING THE ACTORS INTO WHAT THEY ARE NOT. WE ASK THE PUBLIC TO BELIEVE THAT EVERY TIME THEY SEE A PERFORMER ON THE SCREEN HE'S BECOME A DIFFERENT PERSON.
>
> – EDITH HEAD, LEGENDARY HOLLYWOOD COSTUME DESIGNER "

Ready to see if costume design is for you? Try your hand at creating unique costumes for yourself, your friends, or your siblings. Volunteer with the costume department at a local theater.

Investigate costume design programs at art schools, colleges, or universities. During or after college, an internship or apprenticeship will help you gain experience and create valuable networking contacts.

DESIGNING REY'S COSTUME FOR
STAR WARS: THE FORCE AWAKENS

After reading the script for **Star Wars: The Force Awakens,** costume designer Michael Kaplan knew the kind of costume that the character Rey needed. She was poor and worked as a scavenger. The planet was a hot desert. So Kaplan designed versatile dust-colored garments made out of natural materials. The crisscrossed gauze top could be used as a rope or pulled up to keep sand out of her eyes. The tunic could keep her warm or be wrapped around her head to keep her hair out of her face. Rey's goggles, if you look closely, appear to be made out of old Stormtrooper headgear. The earth color identified her as part of the Rebel force. A flowing scarf, signifying the exciting movements to come, flaps behind her in the first scene. Every detail in Rey's costume tells the story of this exciting new character.

REY'S WAX STATUE AT MADAME TUSSAUDS

At a Glance

The basics: Costume designer

Also known as: Costume attendant

At a glance: Costume designers are responsible for the overall look of the clothes and costumes in live performance, film, or television productions.

Education/skills required: Bachelor's degree in fashion design or fashion merchandising

Suggested courses: Art, clothing design and sewing, computer-assisted design (CAD), drawing and painting, textiles, history, literature, introduction to business

Salary range: $19,570–$91,440/year

Median salary: $21.40/hour or $44,500/year

Be prepared for some challenges with this career. Costume design work can be seasonal. Jobs may only last a few weeks or months. You may have to move to a large city to find TV, film, or theater work. But if the idea of transforming a person into a character in a whole different world is irresistible to you, then costume design may be a perfect career.

CHAPTER 10
Boutique Owner

Are you a determined shopper looking to express your own unique sense of style? If so, you have probably discovered the magic of boutiques. These stores truly reflect the individuality of their owners. The word *boutique* is French for *shop*, however, it was in swinging 1960s London, not Paris, that boutiques earned their mod reputation. They fed a new desire for clothes that were fun, affordable, and unique.

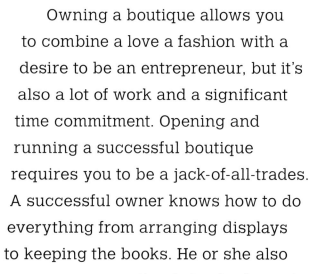

Owning a boutique allows you to combine a love a fashion with a desire to be an entrepreneur, but it's also a lot of work and a significant time commitment. Opening and running a successful boutique requires you to be a jack-of-all-trades. A successful owner knows how to do everything from arranging displays to keeping the books. He or she also attends trade shows to purchase inventory.

A successful boutique owner is likely a people person. To keep the store up and running you'll need some important people skills, such as managing your employees, motivating them to do their best, and resolving any conflicts that arise. You'll also need to know your customers — especially what they can and will buy. For instance, you may want to attract young adult workers who need professional clothes. You may focus on a small area, such as high-fashion shoes or handmade jewelry.

There's more to owning a boutique than just shopping and knowing trends. As a boutique owner, you'll also need a background in business. You will be actively involved in ordering inventory, keeping the books, paying your employees, and managing the store. You may need to get a loan from a bank to start the boutique.

FAST FASHION

If you are like many teens, you love to shop at stores such as H&M and Forever 21. The clothes are trendy and inexpensive. But are they environmentally friendly? Some fashion critics call these clothes "fast fashion." Fast fashion clothes follow new fads, but fads change quickly. Clothes end up only being worn for a short time before being discarded — many end up in landfills. Critics recommend consumers recycle the clothes — or better yet, avoid fast fashion altogether. Instead of following the latest trends, buy well-made clothes designed to last. Set your own trend of thinking about the environment instead of the latest new top or skirt.

> " IF YOU EVER THOUGHT OF OWNING YOUR OWN BOUTIQUE, IT WOULD HELP TO KNOW HOW TO RUN A STORE FIRST. WORKING FOR A CORPORATE CHAIN OR FRANCHISE NOT ONLY GIVES YOU THE EXPERIENCE OF RUNNING A SHOP, IT ALSO HELPS YOU DEVELOP A BIRD'S-EYE-VIEW OF HOW THE INDUSTRY OPERATES.
>
> — JIAN DELEON, FORMER EDITOR AT COMPLEX MEDIA "

More and more boutique owners are using the Internet and social media to gain customers. You may decide to have an online presence. That way you can make sales to customers outside your area. Your boutique may be entirely online, eliminating the need to pay for a physical space other than a warehouse for storing the inventory. However, you will need to buy and learn to use online tools, such as creating and maintaining a website, taking payment, and shipping sold items.

At a Glance

The basics: Boutique owner

Also known as: Entrepreneur

At a glance: Boutique owners purchase inventory, hire and manage employees, keep the accounts, negotiate property leases, and market and sell merchandise.

Education/skills required: Bachelor's degree in business or accounting recommended

Suggested courses: Accounting, banking and finance, computer applications, economics, introduction to business, marketing, statistics

Salary range: $20,000–$130,000/year

Median salary: $49,437/year

Boutique owners don't necessarily need a college degree, however, courses in fashion, accounting, and business are useful. If you think being a boutique owner would be the perfect career, try getting a job in one first. This would be a great way to get work experience. You can find out if owning a boutique is the right career for you.

STARTING AN ONLINE VINTAGE BOUTIQUE

These days anyone can become a boutique owner. The Internet makes it easy for fashionistas with a little money and a lot of ambition and time. All it takes is an account with an online marketplace such as Etsy or eBay. Here are the steps to creating an online vintage shop.

1. **Find your inventory** —This means going to thrift stores, flea markets, and garage sales. Look for pieces that are in good condition. On Etsy, vintage means at least 20 years old.

2. **Set prices** — Compare your items to other items online to set a fair price. It helps if you can put a date on an item. Look in old online catalogs for a match to your pieces. Customers may pay more for authentic clothing from the 1950s or 1960s.

3. **Take detailed photographs** — Use a model or a mannequin so customers can see how it looks on. If you use a model, don't show his or her face, to protect privacy.

4. **List measurements, not sizes** — Sizing has changed over the years. You don't want your customers unhappy because the clothes don't fit.

5. **Use social media** — Social media apps are a great place to advertise your items. Starting a blog can also help customers find you.

6. **Ship the clothes** — As soon as the order comes in, get your clothes packed up and sent to buyers ASAP. Keep on looking for new items to sell.

CHAPTER 11

Get Ready for Your Future!

The fashion world is a huge industry with many options for careers behind the glitz and glamour of the runway or camera. But how do you know which direction to take when planning your career? Think about how you would answer these questions.

1. What are your best subjects in school?
   - Art: Consider display, costume design, or photography.
   - English: Think about a career in fashion writing.
   - Math: The business side of fashion might be for you.
2. What are your personality strengths?
   - I'm confident and outgoing.
     - Consider marketing and public relations.
   - I'm creative and adventurous.
     - Look at being a makeup artist or designer.
   - I'm focused and well organized.
     - Buying or production might be your area.
3. What is your fashion style?
   - I love to rock thrift store finds!
     - You might love creating a unique boutique.
   - I sew my own unique designs.
     - You are on your way to a career as a fashion designer.
   - I shop my way to the latest trends.
     - You would make a great stylist!

66 WHEN YOU SEE AN IMAGE THAT YOU LOVE, RIP IT OUT AND SAVE IT FOR REFERENCE. MAGAZINE COVERS, PICTURES OF PAINTINGS, ADVERTISEMENTS, ANYTHING – COLLECT THEM ALL. WHETHER YOU WANT TO BE A DESIGNER, A STYLIST, A FASHION EDITOR, A MAKEUP ARTIST, OR A PHOTOGRAPHER, THESE IMAGES WILL SERVE AS INSPIRATION TO YOU AS YOUR CAREER PROGRESSES.

– GLORIA BAUME, FORMER FASHION DIRECTOR AT *TEEN VOGUE* 66

Ten tips to get that future started!

1. Learn to sew your own clothes.
2. Take as much math as you can. You will need it when taking measurements or keeping the books at your own boutique.
3. Work at a retail clothing store to learn about clothes and customers.
4. Save money for college.
5. Ask for art, photography, and fashion books for your birthday.
6. Make a fashion lookbook of your favorite designs torn from magazines.
7. Practice photographing your friends in their most creative looks.
8. Create a fashion blog or vlog.
9. Start a fashion club at your school.
10. Practice applying makeup on your friends.

It's easy to dream of being a glamorous supermodel, posing in front of the camera. But the careers behind the camera can be just as exciting. The challenge is to learn as much as you can about them. Find your passion. Nurture your talents and acquire the skills you need. Be ready to work hard and start at the bottom. Mentors in the industry have all been there and are willing to help. Take their advice, and you too can make your dream of a fashion career come true.

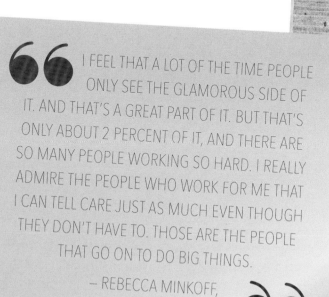

"AROUND SIXTH GRADE, MY MOM AND I FINALLY FOUND A PAIR OF MEN'S JEANS THAT FIT ME WELL. IT WAS AN AMAZING MOMENT TO GO TO SCHOOL WEARING JEANS LIKE MY FRIENDS. EVERYONE WAS COMMENTING ON HOW COOL THEY WERE. THAT'S THE MOMENT I MADE THE CONNECTION BETWEEN FASHION AND SELF-ESTEEM. I BECAME REALLY ADDICTED TO THAT FEELING."

– AIMEE CHESHIRE,
FOUND OF ONLINE SHOP
HEY, GORGEOUS!

 I FEEL THAT A LOT OF THE TIME PEOPLE ONLY SEE THE GLAMOROUS SIDE OF IT. AND THAT'S A GREAT PART OF IT. BUT THAT'S ONLY ABOUT 2 PERCENT OF IT, AND THERE ARE SO MANY PEOPLE WORKING SO HARD. I REALLY ADMIRE THE PEOPLE WHO WORK FOR ME THAT I CAN TELL CARE JUST AS MUCH EVEN THOUGH THEY DON'T HAVE TO. THOSE ARE THE PEOPLE THAT GO ON TO DO BIG THINGS.

– REBECCA MINKOFF,
FASHION DESIGNER

READ MORE

Dallas, Justin, and Rebecca Rissman. *Fashion Photographer.* The Coolest Jobs on the Planet. Chicago: Raintree, 2015.

Gogerly, Liz. *A Teen Guide to Eco-Fashion.* Chicago: Heinemann Library, 2013.

Hennesy, Kathryn, ed. *The Fashion Book.* New York: DK Children, 2014.

Lavergne, Michael. *Fixing Fashion: Rethinking the Way We Make, Market, and Buy Our Clothes.* Gabriola Island, BC, Canada: New Society Publishers, 2015.

Szumsk, Bonnie. *Careers in Fashion.* Exploring Careers. San Diego: ReferencePoint Press, 2014.

INTERNET SITES

Facthound offers a safe, fun way to find Internet sites related to this book. All of the sites on Facthound have been researched by our staff.

Here's all you do:

Visit www.facthound.com

Type in this code: 9781515748977

ABOUT THE AUTHOR

Susan Henneberg is the author of numerous nonfiction books for children, teens, and young adults. As a high school teacher and college instructor for over 30 years, she specializes in books that help students think about careers. She lives and works in Reno, Nevada.

WANT TO LEARN MORE ABOUT
THE CAREERS BEHIND THE SCENES
IN SOME OF THE WORLD'S MOST
GLAMOROUS INDUSTRIES?

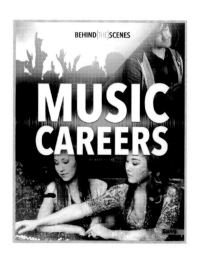
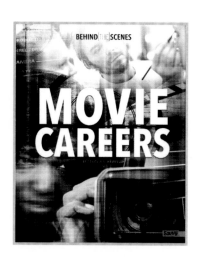

CHECK OUT THESE TITLES TO GO

Behind the Glamour

IN PRO SPORTS, MUSIC, AND MOVIES.